Softly
In
Silver
Sandals

A Selection Of
Writings On Love

By Flavia Weedn

Flavia

APPLAUSE INC.
Woodland Hills, CA 91365-4183
© Flavia Weedn
All Rights Reserved
Special Thanks to All the Flavia Team Members at Applause
Licensed by APPLAUSE Licensing
19898

Library of Congress Catalog Card Number: 89-85001

SOFTLY IN SILVER SANDALS
Printed in Hong Kong
ISBN 0-929632-06-0

*This book is dedicated
to those of you who know
the pure splendour of love —
and who have found the magic
so needed by the heart.*

Flavia

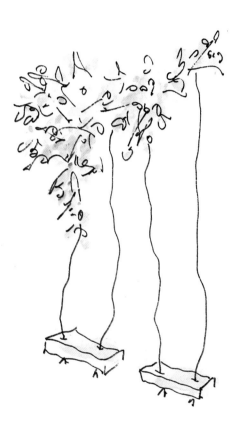

*And
one day
love comes
walking
softly
in
silver sandals
and
steals
our hearts
away.*

◆ ◆ ◆

Love
is the
stardust
from that
first beginning...

*...when
God
scattered
stars
into space.*

   ◆   ◆   ◆

Hearts
will
always
seek hearts
and
love will
come
to those
who
give it.

♦ ♦ ♦

*You
are
my friend,
my love,
my forever
valentine.*

♦ ♦ ♦

Love
develops
deep within
you.
It grows
and is
constantly
changing.

♦ ♦ ♦

Sometimes
there is
someone
who
takes
time enough
to
listen...

*...who
cares about us
when we
lose
and who
loves us
even when
we're wrong.*

◆ ◆ ◆

For all
the times
I never said
the things
I should have,
I thank you
for all
the times
you understood.

◆　◆　◆

Be
patient,
heart.
There are
phantom dreams
and
paper stars
I still
must chase.

◆　◆　◆

Our
deepest
feelings
never
take wing
for they
live
in words
unspoken.

◆ ◆ ◆

*In
some
long ago
time
softly
and
from
afar...*

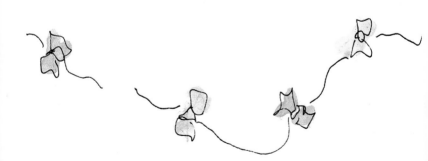

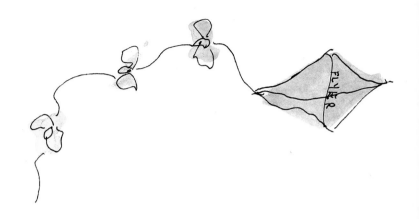

*...I
loved
you
and yet
you
never
knew.*

◆ ◆ ◆

Some
meetings
are
fashioned
by chance.
Ours
was
a gift
of Fate.

♦ ♦ ♦

*You
are magic.
I'm
so glad
you happened
to me.*

◆ ◆ ◆

*What
is more
necessary
than to
love
and
be loved
in return?*

♦ ♦ ♦

There
is
a place
I run to
when
I'm scared
or lonely...

*...I
wonder
if
you
know
the place
is you.*

◆ ◆ ◆

Thank you
for
sharing
my
hopes
and
my hurts.

♦ ♦ ♦

You
are a
prince,
a hero,
a gentle one
who
brings me
Camelot.

◆ ◆ ◆

*Life
is
a gift
tied
with
heartstrings.*

♦ ♦ ♦

*Without love
there
would be
no squeezing
of hands,
no softening
of hurts...*

*...and
there
would be
no eyes
to share
joy
with.*

◆　◆　◆

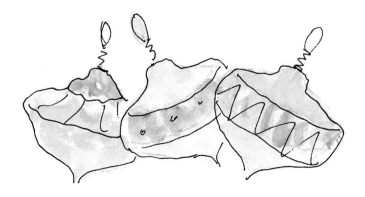

*Hold
a hand
that
needs you
and
discover
abundant
joy.*

❖   ❖   ❖

*Sharing
a life
together
is
sharing
steps
in time...*

*...the music
is different
to each
of us
but
how beautiful
the dance.*

◆ ◆ ◆

*Into
every
heart
comes
pennies
from
Heaven.*

◆   ◆   ◆

If
while
you are
a child
just
one
someone
loves you
uncritically...

*...then
you
will have
love
to give
for
the rest
of your life.*

♦ ♦ ♦

Care
is
the
golden
gift
that
alters
worlds.

♦ ♦ ♦

I
wish you
love
to hold
when you
feel empty
and
a hand
to hold
when
you're afraid.

◆ ◆ ◆

The
human
heart
lives
not
a single
moment
without
the
need
for love.

◆ ◆ ◆

*Each time
I look at
something
I've loved
I realize
the
difference
love
makes
to
our hearts...*

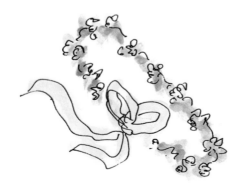

*...and
I know
then
how
lucky
I am
to have
you
in
my life.*

◆ ◆ ◆

And
Fate said,
"Into
each
life
one day
a Prince
shall
come."

♦ ♦ ♦

If
I could
sit
across
the porch
from
God,
I'd thank
Him
for
lending me
you.

♦ ♦ ♦

*You
are the
Princess
in my
fairy tale.
May
I be
your
love?*

◆   ◆   ◆

*Some
people
come
into
our lives
and
quickly go.*

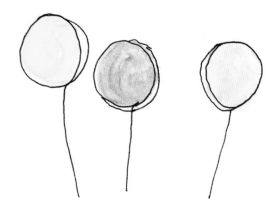

*Some stay
for awhile,
leave footprints
on our hearts
and we
are never, ever
the same.*

♦ ♦ ♦

Thank
you
for
the gifts
you give me;
the
laughter,
the love
and
for being
my
friend.

◆ ◆ ◆

You
put
stars
in
my
eyes.

◆ ◆ ◆

*It
is not
important,
this distance
between us.
Being close
to someone
is an affair
of the
heart.*

❖   ❖   ❖

Today
I saw
a tin soldier
and
a loved-up
doll.
I thought of
other times
and
other places...

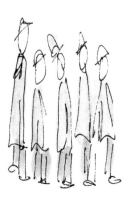

*...of
watermarked
yesterdays
and of
a time
my heart
saved...
a time
with
you.*

♦ ♦ ♦

The
greatest
celebrations
are
anniversaries
of
the heart.

◆ ◆ ◆

*That
you and I
could
live our lives
at the
same time
on earth,
how
incredible
God's plan.*

◆ ◆ ◆

*When
you
love
someone
you prove
you
exist.*

◆   ◆   ◆

*I
remember
the little
things
and times
we've
shared
that made
me happy.*

Thank
you
for
each
and every
moment
you've
given me.

◆ ◆ ◆

Our
hearts
are full
of
treasures
untold.

◆ ◆ ◆

The End

Flavia Weedn is a writer, painter and philosopher. Her life's work is about hope for the human spirit. "I want to reach people of all ages who've never been told, 'Wait a minute, look around you. It's wonderful to be alive and every one of us matters. We can all make a difference if we keep trying and never give up'". It is Flavia and her family's wish to awaken this spirit in each and every one of us. Flavia's messages are translated into many foreign languages, and are distributed worldwide.

For more information about Flavia or to receive the "Flavia Newsletter" write to:
Flavia
Box 42229 • Santa Barbara, CA 93140